Gratitude: A 31 Day Affirmation & Devotional Guide

TAMIEKA SMITH

Gratitude: A 31 Day Affirmation & Devotional Guide

ISBN: 0692659471

ISBN-13: 978-0692659472

DEDICATION

This book was totally something that was not in my plan but I suppose God had other plans. I am so grateful for my Lord and Savior for giving me this vision to create this to have this in the hands of many. I especially want to thank my family and friends for your continuous support in all of my endeavors. To my boys: This is dedicated to you. May God be with you in all of your days. Be bold and confident no matter what this world may tell you. Go with the flow of GOD and you will never fail. I love you!

INTRODUCTION

I'm a firm believer in positive self-talk. Daily we are in a mental war of battling the negative thoughts as we go through our daily lives. This book came to me at a time when I felt that nothing was going right except two things: being a prayer warrior instead of worrier and remaining positive throughout all things no matter what. Having gratitude daily is a way to show appreciation for life. Ever see people that should be giving up but somehow still maintain a smile on their face? It's their positive attitude that keeps them going and their belief system. Before the hustle and bustle, looking at social media, getting the family ready to get caught up in the rat race, what are you saying to yourself when you wake up? Affirming positive thoughts with a devotional scripture is to guide you into a more PURPOSEful life. Enjoy this journey. I've made plenty of space for you to write notes. Remember to always show gratitude throughout your next 31 day journey.

DAY 1

"I know today will be a great day. I am confident with all of my decisions. I choose to be happy."

Knowing that you have the power to do what God called you to do will give you confidence. It makes you feel empowered to take on anything. From Philippians 4:13 (KJV) I can do all things through Christ who strengthens me. You are not strengthened by some things but by all things with confidence. Let go of the second guessing and acknowledge you are worthy of having great days. Command that your day will be great with confidence. Choose to be happy because it expected of you to do so. 1 Thessalonians 5:16-18 (NIV) states to rejoice always, pray continually, give thanks in all circumstances, for this is God's will for you in Christ Jesus. Let go and let God.

7

DAY 1 NOTES

What are you empowered to do today?

DAY 2

"I speak of good things because I am humbly great. My purpose today is to give the world what I have to offer. Someone needs me."

I'm sure you have heard or read this scripture. **Psalm 46:5 (NIV)** God is within her, she will not fall; God will help her at break of day. With the darkness of the night, a new day breaks with new light. The new light symbolizes a new beginning. We always think that a "New Beginning" starts at a new calendar year. The grace of God gives us purpose in each new day. He gave us the duration of time to make decisions within each minute. Yes, his will be done but we cannot pray without works. It is indeed dead.

DAY TWO NOTES

What is your purpose?

DAY 3

"My determination keeps me humble. My perseverance keeps me strong. My grace follows favor in my life."

A grateful person is a happy person. Their gratitude follows them wherever they go. The story of **Ruth 2:10 (KJV)** is a great example of remaining humble in whatever you do. Your hard work will not go unseen. There could be endless of opportunities at your feet by who you could consider a stranger (Boaz). There are no mistakes. Stay humble with your walk and your works will be recognized among many. A stranger will recognize greatness within you. Be determined to be great in all of your days.

DAY 3 NOTES

In what ways are you grateful?

DAY 4

"I am confidently walking in the right direction of my life."

When you are confident enough to know that God's will shall be done in all ways daily, we are surrendering our own plans to let him lead. Do you know where you want to be? It feels great when you know where you are going. When you are lost, it's frustrating, confusing, tiresome, and even create feelings of abandonment.God knows what is best for you more than anyone else. Be confident to know that. **Proverbs 3:5-6 (KJV)** tells us, "Trust in the LORD with all your heart, and lean not on your own understanding. In all your ways acknowledge him." So today trust in him with ALL of your heart in good and bad times. With each new day there is a promise of something great.

DAY 4 NOTES

Have you ever tried doing things without God? If so have you decided to make a change? List ways to let God spiritually move you in the right direction of your life.

DAY 5

"I am whole in my life. The things I hope for will come abundantly."

God created you whole with the proper equipment. We at times need the right tools to use as a guide as we excel into our desires. **Psalm 128:2 (NIV)** You will eat the fruit of your labor; blessings and prosperity will be yours. Fret not of any circumstances that you face. Do not worry about what that family member, friend, coworker, or even a spouse has to say about the anointing that God has over your life. He is testing your faith even where people you love doubt your abilities. Don't get upset at them. The tricks of the enemy will even go through your closest loved ones. These are the times where you fervently hold on to your faith and keep working with wholeness into the desires of your heart.

DAY FIVE NOTES

How are you created whole in the image of God?

DAY 6

"I speak with authority and people of authority is working in my favor."

The words that we speak are so valuable. It is said that the power lies life and death in the power of the tongue. However in the scripture specifically, death and life are in the power of the tongue: and they that love it shall eat the fruit thereof. **Proverbs 18:21 (KJV)**. Think about your interactions today. The words that you say can bring light and life to someone. It can also do the opposite. Words can destroy a person's spirit. If someone is attacking you, don't look at that person. Their spirit could be broken. The best thing for you to do is speak life even when, especially when attacked It's so easy to clapback, but don't. Joyfully speak kind words out to the world. People of authority will come forward to be your cheerleaders. Don't be surprised if they are strangers.

DAY 6 NOTES

Life and death are in the power of the tongue. How are you using your words positively or negatively?

DAY 7

"My gift to the world is unique."

It's okay to stand out from the crowd. You are wonderfully created whole. I'm sure you've heard of the Parable of Talents. In **Matthew 25:14-30** the servants was given an assignment. The obedient one saw that their talents (money) multiplied. Then there was one. The stubborn one not willing to do something different. He could not allow to see how given this currency could bless him tenfold and decided to bury it. Being disobedient only blocked his blessing. What are you burying? Why are you afraid to do what you are assigned to do? Today I leave you with another verse **Luke 6:38 (NIV)**. Give, and it will be given to you. A good measure, pressed down, shaken together and running over, will be poured into your lap. For with measure you use, it will be measured to you. God gave you a gift for harvest. It's time to use it.

DAY SEVEN NOTES

What gifts do you have to offer the world?

DAY 8

"Prosperity is within me and around me."

Command that today you will flourish in a mighty way. Everything around you will bloom beautifully. You know the saying you reap what you sow? Sow doesn't always mean financially. Build someone else up. If it's you that needs building, be humble enough to receive it. God knows what he has in store for us. **Jeremiah 29:11 (NIV)** states, for I know the plans I have for you, declares the LORD, plans to prosper you and not to harm you, plans to give you hope and a future. Shalom is a Hebrew word not only for peace but also for prosperity. Today I pray that you are of peace and sound mind full of prosperity. Shalom.

DAY EIGHT NOTES

In what ways are you already prosperous?

DAY 9

"Miracles are happening with supernatural leaps and bounds."

Today you will be raised. Whatever had you bound yesterday, command it right now to GO! You are not what the enemy told you. God is in the blessing business. He healed the beggar unable to walk. **Acts 3:7-10 (KJV)**, "Then he seized the man's right hand with a firm grip and raised him up. And at once his feet and ankles became strong and steady, and with a leap he stood up and began to walk; and he went into them, walking and leaping and praising God. All the people saw him walking and praising God; and they recognized him as the very man who usually sat *begging* for coins at the Beautiful Gate of the temple, and they were filled with wonder and amazement and were mystified at what had happened to him. If God can do that for him, why you think he can't do that for you?

DAY 9 NOTES

What supernatural blessings are you commanding in your life?

DAY 10

"I am going to start my day with open enthusiasm."

Let's face it. Daily it can be a struggle to be positive. Our first thoughts in the day start as soon as we wake. The enemy immediately comes in trying to bring in negative self-talk. When this occurs, it is important to reinforce positive thoughts. No matter the series of events that lead up to a bad day, remember it's just a day. It will pass. Maintain enthusiasm in spite of. **Ecclesiastes 7:14 (NIV)**, "When times are good, be happy, but when times are bad, consider this: God has made the one as well as the other. Therefore, no one can discover anything about their future." Today is the day that the LORD has made. I will rejoice and be glad in it.

DAY TEN NOTES

With every negative thought, it is great to have a positive thought. List some of your own uplifting scriptures.

DAY 11

"With every waking moment, I know the power I hold within. I am the answer to someone's prayer."

From the moment you wake up God is blessing you with a gift. Today is a day to recognize your strength without any doubt in your mind about your abilities. Someone needs what you have to offer to the world. In **Ephesians 3:20 (AMP)**, "Now to Him who is able to [carry out His purpose and] do superabundantly more than all that we dare ask or think [infinitely beyond our greatest prayers, hopes, or dreams], according to His power that is at work within us." Don't be afraid to ask fervently for what it is you desire. Fervent means having a passionate intensity. Be intentional about your purpose with passion.

DAY 11 NOTES

What are your fervent desires?

Get some scriptures together that confirms the promises of God. Get to praying!

DAY 12

"My words are sweet like honey. They speak life over me."

We spoke about how powerful our words can be on Day 6. Today, look at it from a different approach. Ever said something so foolish it was too late to take it back? Regretfully we say things to others out of hate, anger, or frustration. Once we say them we can end up hurting someone close to us. Think of how you felt when someone said something to you and immediately brightened your day. How easy it is to forget the impression we leave with others? Today the mission is to put a smile on someone's face. **Ecclesiastes 10:12 (AMP)**, "The words of a wise man's mouth are gracious *and* win him favor, but the lips of a fool consume him." What are you consuming today? Favor or foolishness?

DAY 12 NOTES

What are you speaking life of today? Favor or foolishness?

DAY 13

"A new day springs renewal. I decree this will be a great day."

As much as we like to be in control of everything, it can be a challenge letting God's will to be done. REALLY letting his will be done means letting go of how we think things should go then allowing them to be done at His time. Submission is a sign of strength. **Luke 22:42 (NIV)**, "Father, if you are willing take this cup from me: yet not my will, but yours will be done." Jesus knew of the suffering to come but regardless of what was approaching he still was not of his own will. Decree today will be a great day. When you decree a thing you are carrying out an order. Declaring it is manifesting it on Earth as you speak it out in the atmosphere. **Matthew 6:10**, "Thy Kingdom come, Thy will be done on earth, as it is in heaven **(KJV)**." Today will be a great day because you think it and command it to be by His will.

DAY 13 NOTES

In Job 22:28 (KJV) Thou shalt decree a thing, and it shall be established unto thee: and the light shall shine upon my ways. Create your own declarations over your life.

DAY 14

"I will walk into this new day with a fearless and bold spirit."

Confidently go where you are directed without doubt. Know that with each new day something is working in your favor. Don't be afraid of what's ahead of you because he will direct you in all of your ways from **Proverbs 3:6 (KJV)**. Things are behind you for a reason. No need to ever be anxious about the future. The life we live is to remove fear, self-doubt and any second guessing. Faith and fear simply doesn't go together. Stop waiting to live. Stop waiting for someone to say what is on your mind. Stop living for other people. God made you in his image to move with confidence. Stand out from the crowd.

DAY 14 NOTES

Faith and fear simply cannot coexist. What three things are you going to be bold about? Or simply just start out with one. Write them down and post them where you can see it daily.

DAY 15

"I leave fear behind me. Confidence is in front of me."

Why must we continue to walk in fear? So many of us are what I like to call "scary Christians". We get so caught up in the what ifs, this could happen, or that could happen. The next thing you know it paralyzed you. One month went by, then two, then three years of sitting on what God has ordained for you to do. In **2 Timothy 1:7 (KJV)** it states, "For God hath not given us the spirit of fear, but of power, and of love, and of sound mind." You know what gives us fear? The spirit of the enemy. It wants you to feel powerless. Recognize the power within you. Stop allowing the self doubt to get to you in your mind. Be bold enough to try.

DAY 15 NOTES

What things are you going to be bold enough to try? Do the research and stop procrastinating on the things that you have put in your "what if" list. Now we are at the halfway mark on your journey. Keep striving forward. No looking back!

DAY 16

"Wealth abounds in every aspect of my life."

A poor mindset is worse than a poor wallet. The thoughts you possess are powerful more than you can imagine. **Isaiah 55:8-9 (AMP)** tells us that, "For my thoughts are not your thoughts, Nor are your ways my ways, declares the Lord. For as the heavens are higher than the Earth, So are my ways higher than your ways and my thoughts higher than your thoughts." The thoughts of man can be limited whereas the thoughts of God holds no bound and are limitless. God doesn't think like man; because he knows our weaknesses. Rest assured when you think positive thoughts, abide in His word, and complete the assignments given to you, there is no room for failure. He will give you the desires of your heart if you just trust in him. **Psalm 37:4 (NIV)**

DAY 16 NOTES

Today look up some financial prosperity scriptures. Use sticky notes where you will see them on a regular basis. Read them out loud when you wake up and when you go to sleep. God wants you healthy. Claim your inheritance.

DAY 17

"Today and everyday of my life has purpose."

God has a purpose for everyone. Even you. Sometimes it may feel like, "Lord, why me?" It is imperative to reposition your thoughts. Why not you? Read this excerpt from **Exodus 9:16 (ESV)** "But for this purpose I have raised you up, to show you my power, so that my name may be proclaimed in all the earth." What is your divine assignment? Think about the goals you wish to accomplish. There is no greater time than now to fulfill your dreams. Another word for today is **Romans 8:28 (KJV)** And we know that all things work together for good to those who love God, to those who are called according to *His* purpose.

DAY 17 Notes

Today is a reflection of where you are. Do you know what your divine assignment is? Ask God for an encounter for confirmation. Fasting is a great way to allow him to come in. Personally, I fast on Tuesdays. If your request requires more, perhaps a 3, 7 or 21 day fast may be better suited.

DAY 18

"The things that I have learned are tools for teaching."

Experience is the best teacher. Sometimes when we go through some of the most worst things in our lives, it is hard to find a way to make sense out the situation. The best way is to think of it as a student turning into a teacher. In **John 13:14**, "So if I, the Lord and the Teacher, washed your feet, you ought to wash another's feet as well." If he was humble enough to wash his disciples feet and being prophetic to acknowledge they wasn't clean, why can't you do the same for your brother or sister? The washing of feet wasn't in a literal sense in this scripture. It's to humbly serve and teach another. Your own story can be used for testimony as a way to teach others not to make the same mistakes as you. Iron sharpens iron and it is our duty to sharpen the next person.

DAY 18 Notes

Everyone has teachable life experiences that they can share to another. How can your experiences impact the world?

DAY 19

"I work in preparation for everything I pray for."

Confessing is apart of making your requests known to God. He hears us wholeheartedly. In Luke **6:45 (NLT)** it tells us that, "What you say flows from what is in your heart." In the preparation of the things we pray for we also have to work for them. Imagine going to the parking lot of a car dealership and telling the sales agent with a straight face, "Yes I will take that sports car over there." And you have no means to finance it. You would get laughed at. That's how God looks at you when you request the things you want without due diligence. But the caveat is doing the work. Faith without works is dead **(James 2:17 NIV)**. You are being tested before claiming that goal. Before acing the test you have to prepare and study. Work that way towards any new level you are requesting in your life.

Day 19 Notes

Write down some of your desires. After completing, decide the steps you will take to make them come into fruition. Our "To Do" lists include becoming our better selves by accomplishing goals the right way. Using patience, diligence, and obedience.

DAY 20

"Someone needs what I have to say today."

Words of encouragement can mean the world to another person. The timing of a good word is having confirmation of what could be on another's heart. Therefore encourage one another and build each other up, just as you are doing. **1 Thessalonians 5:11 (NIV)** Allow your unique insight on the world offer a light of hope to the people around you today. Words are incredibly impactful to another. Just like when you hear a great speech, it calls you to action in one way or another. In a world that cast shadows, help one of out the wilderness. A voice called out in the wilderness, Prepare a way for the Lord, make straight paths for him. **Mark 1:3 (NIV).** John the Baptist was a messiah preached to those in the wilderness about the good news of the Lord. Imagine your words delivering someone from their own wilderness.

Day 20 Notes

Today challenge is to offer kind words to someone that needs it. Tell someone how much they mean to you. Small acts of kindness goes a long way.

DAY 21

"I am a winner. Today is a day to win."

A champion has the mindset to win before getting on the field. That is the first of training. Your mental ability has to always be strong. Confessing defeat is confessing failure to win. Change the perspective of your thoughts. The negative self talk has a root deep down because someone may have told you something a long time ago that may have unconsciously stuck around. It convinced you to actually believe it. Let that go and be triumphant. But you are a chosen people, a royal priesthood, a holy nation, God's special possession, that you may declare the praises of him who called you out of the darkness into his wonderful light. **1 Peter 2:9 (NIV)**

Day 21 Notes

Write down at least 5 positive things to say when doubt comes in your mind.

DAY 22

"The pain of yesterday is behind me. Today is a day of renewed happiness."

Being hurt can leave scars that can last a lifetime. What it can also leave are lessons. Joy is never dependent on any circumstance. Mercy, peace, and love be yours in abundance. **Jude 1:2 (NIV).** The life you live is imperfectly perfect. The wrongdoing of others shall not block your joy. Make a declaration today to move beyond the pain of yesterday. Bless those who persecute you. Bless and do not curse. **Romans 12:14 (NIV).**

Day 22 Notes

The exercise for today to have your own set of declarations. Start it off by writing, "On this day I declare…" You can make it as unique as you like. Or you can use this.

On this day, I declare that no weapons formed against me shall prosper. I know who I am and whose I am. The assignment God created for me is to exceedingly, abundantly, and above all things succeed today and everyday.

DAY 23

"Confidently I will decree and declare my blessings in advance."

Speaking about the goodness of the desires of your heart is making an announcement of your thoughts. Call those things as though they are! Claim what's yours before receiving it. God bless those who believe. As it is written, "I have made you the father of many nations,- in the presence of God in whom he believed, who gives life to the dead and calls into existence the things that do not exist. **Romans 4:17 (ESV)**

Day 23 Notes

Today we're practicing speaking things as though they already are. Biblically speaking, the number 7 is the foundation of God's word. It is the number of completion. What are 7 things you will speak of in advance?

DAY 24

"I will reach out to the people that need me."

When someone asked you to do something, what is the immediate response? Do you do it or come up with a million excuses? Life has everyone busy. But what is 5 minutes of dedication just to let someone vent? Or another 10 to give that same person some encouraging words of advice? Let us hold fast the confession of our hope without wavering, for he who is promised is faithful. And let us consider how to stir up one another to love and good works, not neglecting to meet together, as is the habit of some, but encouraging one another, and all the more as you see the Day drawing near. **Hebrews 10:23-25 (NIV)**

Day 24 Notes

The task for today is to unbusy yourself for someone else. Yes, unbusy. Dedicated and people that are willing to serve another are successful people. They realized how virtuous it is to allow a part of them to be present in another's life. That is a Godly gift.

DAY 25

"Regardless of how God may raise me up, I shall remain humble."

When you have a divine assignment on your life, things happen as you "level up". New friends come, lifestyles change, and doors open up that haven't before. Then something else could also happen. An unlimited supply of your ego being fed to you. Never become that person. Put the fork down. Always have people around that will keep it real with you and keep you grounded. Get rid of "Yes" men/women. It's dangerous company. Blessed are the meek; for they shall inherit the earth. **Matthew 5:5 (KJV)**

Day 25 Notes

There are many references in the Bible to tells us to examine our ways. Take note of **Haggai 1:5-6 (NIV)** Now this is what the LORD Almighty says: "Give careful thought to your ways. You have planted much, but harvested little. You eat, but never have enough. You drink, but never have your fill. You put on clothes, but never warm. You earn wages, only to put them in a purse with holes in it." Have an aptitude of gratitude to remain humble in all of your ways.

DAY 26

"The relationships I encounter in my daily life will be watered and flourish."

Having a great friendship is one of the most treasured things on Earth. Relationships of any type should be healthy. It is what makes life rich. Someone with a genuine heart that can be honest with you and it's mutual should be celebrated. The duty of any relationship is to water another. Friendships will grow, some will die but regardless water it while it lasts. Two are better than one because they have a more satisfying return for their labor; for if either of them falls, the one will lift up his companion. But woe to him who is alone when he falls and does not have another to lift him up. **Ecclesiastes 4:9-10 (KJV)**

Day 26 Notes

Today the task is simply water the people around you. It starts with the words you say to the love you show through your actions.

DAY 27

"The transitions of my growth is a teacher for the world around me."

Nothing that you may ever go through is in vain. It is a a collection of lessons that turned into blessings. Remember this: the story you are holding within is a prisoner for two people. The one that's holding it and the one that needs to be set free. Say it without hesitation. It is my pleasure to tell you about the miraculous signs and wonders that the Most High God has performed for me. **Daniel 4:2 (NIV)** Transitions are periods where it can be incredibly uncomfortable. However, it is always for the better. Also know this: "I have planted, Apollos watered, God gave the increase." **1 Corinthians 3:6 (KJV)** In other words, the lesson planted seeds for another to water, so that God gets the increase. Just imagine how something you say can change the direction of a person's life based on what the Holy Spirit planted in you? God continually gives us miracles, signs, and wonders.

Day 27 Notes

In every transition, there is a lesson at the end of each chapter of your life book. Teachers are all around us. At times, we are the students developing into teachable moments. Not all are in the classroom or in the church. Your ministry is all around you. Reflect on the miraculous signs and wonders God has done in your life thus far.

DAY 28

"My work is stewardship for the faith that lies within me."

Take pride in the all the work that you do. Prideful in a way that exudes confidence. Otherwise, it would be false humility. Nothing that you do is because of lack. It is an abundant blessing. Stewardship is an assignment of gratitude. Each one should use whatever gift he has received to serve others, faithfully administering God's grace in various forms. **1 Peter 2:10 (NIV)** Cheerfully serve without complaining. Your serving no matter how big or small is important. Whoever can be trusted with very little can also be trusted with much, and whoever is dishonest with very little will also be dishonest with much. **Luke 16:10 (NIV)**

Day 28 Notes

In what ways are you serving at your best? If it's not where you want it to be, how could you change that?

DAY 29

"Everything I do is for the glory of the kingdom of God."

Everything you do from the moment you wake up is for the glory of God. It is not for raising your name high with the hopes of being accepted or loved by man. Do good works because it is expected of you. Never allow yourself to be spiritually blinded to where you can't hear the voice of God. One day Pharisees asked Jesus, "When will the Kingdom of God come?" Jesus replied, "The Kingdom of God can't be detected by visible signs. You won't be able to say, 'Here it is!', or 'It's over there!' For the Kingdom of God is already among you." **Luke 17:20-21**

Day 29 Notes

Reflect on this scripture: I will give you the keys of the kingdom of heaven, whatever you bind on Earth shall be bound in heaven, whatever you loose on Earth shall be loosed in heaven. **Matthew 16:19**

DAY 30

"Love is within me and it shows in my existence around me."

God is love. How could we say we holy with hatred in our hearts? He did the ultimate sacrifice. For God so loved the World that He gave His only begotten son, that whoever believes in him should not perish but have everlasting life. **John 3:16** Continually, God gives us grace and mercy in our lives. Open up your heart. When one holds hatred, it is a spirit of unforgiveness. Forgive. For we who know Him who said, "Vengeance is Mine, I will repay, says the Lord, And again, "The Lord will judge His people." **Hebrews 10:30**

Day 30 Notes

What are you carrying? Is it love or hatred? Write out your good and bad traits. It's time for a self check. Once you're done, evaluate it. If there more loving attributes, great keep it up. On the other hand, hatred steps root a problem. Find ways to seek help. Pride goes before destruction, a haughty spirit before a fall. **Proverbs 16:18**

DAY 31

"All of my walks on this journey is bringing me closer to my purpose."

Everyday of your life has purpose. The use of gifts should stay and remain active. We have different gifts, according to the grace given to each of us. If your gift is prophesying, then prophesy according to your faith; if it is serving then serve; if it is teaching, then teach; if it is to encourage, then give encouragement; if it is giving, then give generously; if it is to lead, do it diligently; if it is to show mercy, do it cheerfully. **Romans 12:6-8.**

Afterward

Congratulations on your 31 Day journey! I hope each day helped you in some way. As you continue in your daily life of gratitude, I pray continued success to you.

About the Author

From Durham, North Carolina this petite woman used her voice in a strong way by being an advocate and survivor of domestic violence. Her story landed in Huffington Post Woman from her feature in Unconventional Apology. She turned her childhood past time to make writing a living with published works.

She continues her advocacy as an ambassador of 10Blessings. In her spare time she enjoys traveling with her children and trying out new food.

Affectionately called "Ms.Wordsmith" she created Wordsmith Books to sought out her self publishing endeavors to bring words to your world.

Stay connected!

Instagram @TamiekaSmith

Twitter/Periscope @MsWordSmith

For booking information info@tamiekasmith.com

Tamiekasmith.com

Wordsmith Books, LLC

P.O. Box 1858

Apex, NC 27502

Proof

Manufactured by Amazon.com
Columbia, SC
04 April 2017